The Mickey Deegan Poetry Collection

The Mickey Deegan Poetry Collection

Lived and Written by

Mickey Deegan

WORKBOOK PRESS LLC
187 E Warm Springs Rd,
Suite B285, Las Vegas, NV 89119, USA

Website: https://workbookpress.com/
Hotline: 1-888-818-4856
Email: admin@workbookpress.com

Ordering Information:
Quantity sales. Special discounts are available on quantity purchases by corporations, associations, and others. For details, contact the publisher at the address above.

ISBN-13:   000-0-00000-000-0 (Paperback Version)
                     000-0-00000-000-0 (Digital Version)

REV. DATE:

CONTENTS

LIVING A LIFE...

Living a life is hard so it seems,
Believing in wishes, hoping in dreams,
Yes! It's a struggle for something so small,
Sometimes you ask, what means it all?

A face that's often stained with a tear,
A racing heart, that's filled with fear,
A wonderful dream, that falls apart,
Like a game being played, but not so smart,

Living a life, is something different too,
It's knowing, loving and having you,
It's the smile you see, upon my face,
It's being happy to be in the human race.

It's accepting fate, and even pain,
It's loving sunshine, and greeting rain,
It's being thoughtful and sometimes mad,
It's being good and its being bad.

It's wanting peace, yet being able to fight,
It's being weak, and it's displaying might,
It's being independent, but sometimes to reply,
It's being forward and it's being shy.

Yes! Living a Life, is to be in need,
Of fellow men of every creed,
And I know, it must be so very hard,
To live a life... without the help of God.

By Mickey Deegan

"ABANDONED CHILD"

There was a tiny baby girl, who arrived on this cold earth,
Who knows, if anyone celebrated this very special birth,
Her parents gave her up, at the tender age of one,
Of course, she couldn't realize then...... her hell had just begun.

She was sent to an orphanage, then to a foster home,
Facing a long and frightening road, and being all alone,
She remembers the beatings started, when she was only five,
Her life's purpose way back then... was only to survive,

There were nine homes to follow, each more horrible than the last,
Constructing for her, an unforgettable and unspeakable past,
She knew how it felt to be unloved and very insecure,
She knows her faith and belief in God, helped her to endure.

Now she's all grown up, she's taken all the knocks and bruises,
But for the grace of God she's certainly not among the losers,
She's given her very best, to be all that she can be,
You see, I know her story well... that little girl was me.

By Mickey Deegan

"SILENT SINNERS"

This poem is taken form the phrase "To sin by silence,
when you protest, makes cowards of men" said by Abraham Lincoln

loyalty today, seems an old fashion word,
being patriotic, is almost absurd,
America's defenders, appear to be few,
The time to be counted, is certainly due,

There are all kinds of demonstrators, the numbers soar,
Yelling anti government... and anti war,
Terrorists' attacks.... Americans slain,
So many have died... all in vain

Marines attacked in Beirut as they slept,
America grieved and silently wept,
A sailor murdered in a terrorist act
We fought back with tears and political tact,

Injustice on the rampage, a war undeclared,
Decency and patriotism... will not be spared,
It was said our defeat, will be from within,
Not like the past, when we set out to win,

Men went to war, they laid down their life,
Defending America... against foes and strife,
They kept all the enemies away from our shores,
Who's to pick up their banner and carry the cause,

Cowards, dare not raise the flag in display,
Or stand with pride, when it comes their way,
They'll watch injustice, their voice will be still,
They would have us robbed of our freedom and will,

So be counted, show your feelings and pride,

America needs you, now by her side,
Speak for one and all, when there's a wrong,
Let your voice be part of America's song,

Help her stand free... her banner wave,
Remembering too... all who gallantly gave,
Her colors are flying, the red, white and blue,
Because of brave men... Americans like you???

By Mickey Deegan

"THE MARINE MONUMENT"

I stood before a monument, gigantic in size,
I thought the sculptor made one big prize,
I could not believe... a work so great,
I wondered how life... dealt them their fate,

They were the marines, who raised old glory,
Unknown then, it would be a worldwide story,
There atop a hill, they performed their toil,
Raising her high... atop enemy soil,

Their eyes were piercing, yet filled with pride,
"Raised her up" ... I bet their voices cried,
Covering huge muscles, you could see the mud,
They knew to fly her, the price was blood,

On that hill, they stood gallantly brave,
Thinking, of their brothers, they could not save,
Their wrinkled foreheads, were so real life,
You just knew their trouble and their strife,

Dwarfed before this... I held a stone hand,
Wanting them to know, that I did understand,
I thanked them out loud ad was proud of each one,
Me and a nation knew,..... their job was well done.

By Mickey Deegan

"HIS LITTLE FRIEND"

A little boy, about three or four,
Will be as fresh as he can be,
A lot of folks may get real sore,
At that little lad of three,

He may say words, that aren't nice,
And those that hear will scold,
He may be filled with mischievous spice,
But he learned it form the old,

Some folks will look at him and sneer,
As they think, what a hopeless lad,
They may even fill their hearts with fear,
That he'll someday, turn out bad,

They say the age of reason is seven,
So stop and think with a sigh,
That little lad would go right to heaven,
If before then, he should die,

To God, he's an angel, pure as gold,
And free from any sin,
It's examples that are from the old,
That are the best on him,

Though very fresh, as you may think,
He's an angel on this sod,
He's got the very closet link,
To heaven and to God,

God sees his little dirty face,
And thinks of him with joy,
In heaven there is the highest place,
For this mischievous, little boy,

So blame yourself, you older folk,
Think before you sneer,
It's only words, that you have spoke,
That has filled, his little ear,

At night he spends a little while,
And bows in his weary head,
He talks to God with a smile,
Before jumping into bed.

God protects him through the night,
And helps his problems mend,
He knows he'll learn wrong from right,
As He smiles down at "His little friend"

By Mickey Deegan

AMERICA FIRST

Dedicated to Donald Trump

Thank God, the election is over….. and we won,
All the promises Trump has made will be done.
He already got many jobs, taxes lowest in U.S. history,
The people have spoken, and to the liberals it's still a mystery.

What Obama did in eight years was a disgrace,
Or what he didn't do, he was certainly out of place.
Trump now for us will certainly be in the lead,
"America first" will always be in his every deed.

In our trades with countries we gave everything away,
With the new sheriff in town, now they're going to have to pay.
He's going to make everyone do their equal share,
But he insists with all he does, must be very, very fair.

He's going to take care of the wounded and every vet,
He'll do all for them, these rules he already set.
All our children too will be educated, this is a must,
He has their caring also, now they have his trust.

He's going to watch over us, America again will be very strong,
He's going to right all the many, many wrong.
Our ships and airplaines will be repaired or brand new,
This is how he won, and all this he will do.

He doesn't want a war, but won't back down from any foe,
If anyone threatens America, his guts will have to show.
He believes strength means peace, like Americans did before,
That is why America, has won every unwanted and past war.

By Mickey Deegan

"S.S. CROAKER"

Submarine in World War II

Alone and silent, I'm standing here in a cold and misty fog,
Gallantly quiet, but standing tall, with a long and impressive log,

There are the ghosts, of all the men, that shed their blood on me,
They fought with me and bravely died so that you stayed free,

They didn't come back, but I returned and made it to the shore,
Terribly hurt and shaken too, sleeking back from winning a war,

Now you all seem to forget and pass me by, a hero that is faint,
I'm hardly noticed and looking like my chipped and fading paint,

I represent all the galloping ghosts, that roam the seas and moan,
For all the men that died on them forgotten now at home,

I'll stand my watch and keep my position, like they did night and day,
Maybe one day, you'll remember and gratefully glance my way.

By Mickey Deegan

"RYAN"

Dedicated to my grandson

There is a little angel, that came to life,
On a cool night in January, he entered this planet of strife,
Again God has let His perfection known to us,
To make this little angel, how much He had to fuss,

He is perfection, from hishead to his little toes,
With his big, big eyes, right to his tiny little nose,
His pleasant smile, covers his little face,
He makes you feel proud, to be in the human race,

This angel's name is " Ryan", that fits him to a tee,
How very proud I am, that he belongs to me,
You see, I'm his grndma and I thank God, with all my heart,
That in my life, this little angel has become a part,

His Mommy and Daddy are happy too, so his brother Wayne,
In just a couple, of months, he's already reached such fame,
And I know my life and the world is a better place,
Because God has added "Ryan" and his little angel face.

By Mickey Deegan

"TIMMY"

Dedicated to my Son

My heart is broken in constant pain,
Since you have gone away,
Tears falling, like a forever rain,
I carry this with me, each day,

Few know , it hurts much too much,
To talk about your passing,
I shy away from their pity and touch,
With a focus, on the everlasting,

I hope you're in heaven, waiting for me,
That thought, keeps me alive,
Sometimes, I wonder just how it could be,
For so long, that I survived,

So many reminders hurt me so,
Or a certain, familiar place,
I can't help if where I sometimes go,
I see your smiling face,

Your sense of humor caused such joy,
You touched everyone you knew,
Your were such a darling little boy,
Into a handsome man, you grew,

In my locket, each day you're with me,
And you're tucked deep in my heart,
And I know near you'l always be,
Because of me...... you're the greatest part.

By Mickey Deegan

"OUR 37TH PRESIDENT"

Dedicated to President Richard M. Nixon

Americans have faced many crisis before,
Depression, inflation, shortage and war,
Now a different hardship we bear this time,
When 37th president, was forced to resign.

They accused him of wrongdoing….. at Watergate,
For two years we listened to a weary debate,
They hounded and hounded and wouldn't give in,
His enemies together were going, to get him.

Impeachment they cried, long before the proof,
Not really knowing all of the truth,
They turned their backs…. one by one,
Not remembering once, all the good he's done.

He stopped a war…………. We won't forget,
Like the rest of the world, we are in his debt,
For the good he's spread, as he traveled the earth,
Like us, …………. they too, know his worth.

Watergate was wrong and we're very sad,
But at the same time we're fighting mad,
At the democrats and news media, who pushed aside,
The feelings of a nation and walked on its pride.

They shrank from his power and his strength,
They must destroy him at any length,
But millions of Americans and count me as one,
Are pretty damn proud of him, and the job he's done.

By Mickey Deegan

"A JOURNEY'S END"

I've traveled my road, till jourey's end,
I've had success and sorrow... both foe and friend,

I've completed a life and tried my best,
Now, I've gone home forever... for eternal rest,

Weep not for me, go forth, gallant and brave,
Remember ...life started for me at the grave,

Don't feel alone... though you don't see me there,
We'll speak to each other, forever in prayer,

For me, keep smiling, walk sure and tall,
Be of good cheer, bringing comfort to all,

One day you'll be with me, at home here above,
For your strength to go on...... I left you my love.

By Mickey Deegan

"AWFUL POLITICIANS"

*Politics now.... Are getting out of hand,
Hurting and insulting, this great and wonderful land*

*They better stand on their own ground, stay in their own space,
To this country, what they're doing is a real disgrace*

*They're making the word politician, a real dirty word
Everything they're doing is getting awful and absurd*

*We the people are fed up, with their many fight,
Half of them are stupid, with no real insight.*

*They'll attack any group, without caring what they are about,
If they're not on their political side, then they count them out,*

*They'll harass them, through every act and every deed,
All they care about is, they're not the ones in the lead.*

*I wish the American people, will be rea and very strong,
Let them be brave and right this very very wrong,*

*Let the USA be back, when the people were first,
Rid the kind of politicians, that couldn't be worst.*

*Let's remember the people...... are on the real side,
Loving their country and waving their flag with pride,*

*Let the politicians know.... We'll do it all our way,
We'll stay with God, with all our hearts, for the country we will pray.*

By Mickey Deegan

"OUR YESTERDAYS"

I remember the years, now gone past,
As I think of the youthful glee,
I didn't know then, how very fast,
They would get away from me,

Sometimes I'd like to reach right out,
And grab them in my hand,
Sometimes I'd like to even shout,
For those years gone by so grand,

We all have years, which we turn to look,
We think of them with a sigh,
Like the pages tucked away in a book,
Are those wonderful days gone by,

What brings them back and opens the door,
A picture a song or two,
The years that won't return any more,
Now how they seem so few,

Or maybe a letter, with words so worn,
That we try so hard to see,
Maybe a poem, that's slight torn,
Stirs up our memory,

It could be a picture, we chanced to gaze,
As we tidied up a drawer,
This has helped, lift time haze,
As we think of the clothes we wore,

Perhaps it is that certain smile,
A stranger used so free,

It makes us stop and linger awhile,
Of the way life used to be,

Keep your dreams and have happiness to give,
Let tears and sorrows fade,
For every minute of each day you live,
A memory is being made,

Press real tight, to your heart,
The present and all its' ways,
For all too soon, it too will depart,
And tomorrow, will be yesterdays.

By Mickey Deegan

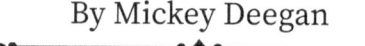

"A MESSAGE FOR AMERICA"

Dedicated to President Ronald Reagan

I've been here now for a little while,
It's calm, peaceful and bright,
Always surrounded, by a warm smile,
Beyond words, it's a beautiful sight,

Rewarded I am, for my job on earth,
He told me, it was well done,
Now I know and realize it's worth,
I tried, but not always I won,

He's generally pleased with the country I love,
And the folks of the United States,
He watches you all, from above,
But He can also,… see the hates,

He loves His children, both white and black,
For some He show despair,
He hopes they find the love thy lack,
As He silently watches there,

He told me too, He was very sad,
As the decision and court rule,
Disappointed in the people it made glad,
For banning His name from school,

He speaks to me often, about America's woes,
The good and the bad, your doing,
He watches too, your many foes,
Everyday all this,…. He's viewing,

You'll be happy to know we've been right along,
The communists are His foe too,
He hopes someday, they'll see their wrong,
And love Him the way you do,

I know, you'll always do your best,
To keep love and justice in the lead,
This He said He would always bless,
And guide you in your hour of need,

So keep America strong and all men free,
Bring peace to that troubled sod,
You'll find everlasting reward like me,
When you too, can walk and talk with God.

By Mickey Deegan

"REFLECTIONS"

Dedicated to Kay Jordan's Cabaret

Sitting at the bar, for a moment serene,
How very strange, it now all seems,
Unwillingly... I become lost in the past,
Thinking of the good times, that never last.

If only the mirrors could say, what they know,
Of all the people, that come and go,
Friends and their laughter, that filled the room,
Now seem to fill me, with a certain gloom.

So many are missed, that are no longer here,
I can't help but think of them, with a tear,
I'll drink to them and the times we shared,
I often wonder how others have fared.

They met and married, and went toward the sun,
I remember the laughs... and all the fun,
A favorite song... has brought back too,
Cherished memories of a certain few.

Let me raise my glass, in a private toast,
And silently remember, with a bit of a boast,
I've met some great people here in this bar,
That have come from near and very far.

Cherished "Reflections" ... mirrors with a key,
Unlocked them for a while... and shared them with me.

By Mickey Deegan

"THAT"S AN AMERICAN"

It's loving this country, far and wide,
With it's skies and rivers, so blue,
It's the way you're always busting with pride,
Because you know, she's part of you,

It's knowing you'll fight, if she's in need.
For she's the home of the brave,
You want her always to be in the lead,
May her colors, always proudly wave,

It's enjoying the gift, bestowed on you,
Holding your head real high,
It's cherishing dear, the red, white and blue
For her you'd be willing to die,

It's respecting others, their countries too,
It's extending a friendly hand,
Especially to those, not as fortunate as you,
Who don't have such a blessed land,

It's keeping her laws and in them abide,
With justice for one and all,
When this is threatened, it's taking her side,
That makes you walk straight and tall,

It's believing in God and asking His aid,
In the conquest, of all her foe,
It's not being ashamed, that they know we prayed
On this land, His blessings bestow,

It's being meek and always fair,
Except to a definite wrong,

It's having might, beyond compare,
Keeping her safe and strong,

She's truly the land of liberty,
There's a welcome on her door,
That's what American, means to me,
For both the rich and poor

By Mickey Deegan

BESTFRIEND

I was very lonely, didn't know what to do,
I had some acquaintances, but they were very few,
Nothing changed the days seemed the very same,
Nothing new happened and nobody new came,

The one day I took a walk, looking all around,
Not knowing how or where I'd be bound,
Walking all alone, I guess that's how it will be,
Suddenly I felt something or someone following me.

I turned to take a look being a little unaware,
Knowing who or what, I might see there.
First I looked up and then I looked down
There was a dog , with a tiny little frown.

He kept followig me not knowing where to go,
Right back to my home, that I was glad to show
That was 5 years ago, he proved to be the best
Protecting me, loving me, loyal and all the rest.

I never felt alone again, I got so much to share,
Back then I searched for an owner, which I couldn't bear.
But he was mine, no one came to take him away,
I'll never forget when, I got my bestfriend, on that lucky special day.

By Mickey Deegan

"WOULD YOU"

Would you be to me, both lover and friend,
Travel the same road... till journey's end,
Would you understand, all the things deep inside,
Stand by me faithfully... stand by with pride?

Would you share all my moments... both happy and sad,
My silly foolishness, and tolerance when mad,
Not only my small victories, but when I've lost,
Would you be right there... at any cost,

Would you be considerate and always kind,
My happiness always... first on your mind,
Would you be willing... life's riches to share,
Not only tell me... but to show me you care,

Would you give me your strength, gentle and tall,
If along life's way, I stumble and fall,
Would you be all these things and never betray my trust,
Then forever to love you,......... this is a must.

By Mickey Deegan

"WAYNE"

Dedicated to My Grandson

We awaited your arrival so anxiously,
Then the day had finally come,
We knew you were going to be a little "he",
A precious and tiny... little one.

But you had topped our wildest dream,
To be so perfect in every way,
A little bundle of peaches and cream,
The 27th of January... was the day.

A touch of heaven was sent from above,
As your surrounded by all of us,
You were certainly made, with a whole lot of love,
Just to see you... explains all the fuss.

God performs all kinds of miracles we know,
But He had to work overtime on you,
A perfect art, from head to toe,
There... in your blanket of blue.

You're a picture that's beyond compare,
With your cute little button nose,
Your wondrous eyes and dark hair,
And cheeks... like petals form a rose.

May you always be surrounded with love,
And protected from all harm,
I know God is watching from above,
And smiling down... at "His little charm".

By Mickey Deegan

THE RED, WHITE AND BLUE

I have been carried on land and sea,
I've been hoisted on many a shore,
I've been surrounded; by men, who fought gallantly,
And was victorious in very war.

Sometimes I really got badly shattered,
My colors were faded and torn,
In many a battle, I was battered,
Sometimes............ I seemed so forlorn.

But I was always lifted....... above it all,
I was protected by the very brave,
I flew proudly always standing tall,
My colors s gallantly wave.

So many lives were given and blood was shed,
So that I will always stay free,
Sadly it took many wounded and dead.
For their love and respect for me.

Cowards now attacked me, on my homeland,
Hoping to destroy what I stand for,
They only made me, much more grand,
Now you'll see' me, on most everyone's door.

Those' cowards don't know, they aren't aware,
Of what all my brave heroes will do,
They'll fight and they'll win, if anyone dare,
Threaten me,........ THE RED, WHITE AND BLUE.

By Mickey Deegan

DEMOCRACY THREATENED

A sneak attack, on the red, white and blue,
Has left us, in shock and in tears,
We ask God's help, to get us through,
And help conquer, our anxieties and fears.

We have an enemy, that must be beat,
They strike civilians and building so tall,
But we have vowed, they'll never defeat,
America,....... As we answer our country's call.

Grief and sorrow and tear filled faces,
As deaths keep mounting more and more,
We search for the enemy in all places,
Now we've been forced to settle a score.

We let our guard down, we've been so free,
Their sneak attacks, have put us on alert,
Shoulder to shoulder we stand,.... for democracy,
We'll rub their faces in their condemnable dirt.

Divided we fall, united we stand,
We're proving that, as you look around,
Patriotism, has loudly stuck up the band,
With flags displayed on houses and ground.

God help us in our fight and days ahead,
Stand by us..... is our request in prayer,
Bless our heroes and embrace our dead,
As our country readies..... with arms to bear.

This....., they started, but they should have known,
This IS THE LAND OF THE FREE.... AND VERY BRAVE,
They've got to be taught, they've got to be shown,
Our red white and blue.... shall... always wave.

By Mickey Deegan

"AMERICA UNDER SIEGE"

I always thought of my country, with such pride,
We fought and won many wars, with allies by our side,
We stood for democracy and answered calls of distress,
We helped where we were needed and wouldn't settle for less,

Now we're in a war with cowardly terrorists, but some don't agree,
That we should be helping…. and setting people free,
We're fighting in a far off land; our military are heroes one and all,
Each one volunteered and proudly answered their country's call,

Another war is being fought, right here in the U.S.A.,
Treasonous foes trying to tear us down in all they do and say,
They start with God, attacking all religions, they would like to ban,
They don't like schools pledging to our flag and a patriotic stand,

They misquote our constitutions and traditions that made this
country great,
They spread violence and mistrust daily, preaching all their hate,
They would like to see us lose the Iraqi war, just to prove us wrong,
Knocking our country, government and military, like they've done all along,
They have tried to hurt us long enough, our patriotism they despise,
So let us stand and be counted, the silent majority has to rise,

We'll stand together, God by our side and flying the red, white and blue,
To pick up the banner and show our strength, this battle is long overdue,
With God's help, we'll take America back, to where she ought to be,
Rid of all foes, her flag flying high Americans… with loyalty!

By Mickey Deegan

BRITTNEY

She was someone special, on this earth,
It was twenty-three years, since her birth,
In those years, she touched all she knew,
She was so special and so loved too.

Being with her and her constant smile,
Made you content, for the special while,
We all miss her, she had to go home,
This life we live, is just a loan.

She too loved all… especially Ryan her love,
To keep him going, she's sending strength from above,
Her family too, she's watching them there,
She's receiving their love, in every prayer.

The flower that's picked, is the most beautiful one,
That is Brittney… and after all is done,
We'll all be together again… when we leave this sad,
Back to our home… with Brittney and with God.

By Mickey Deegan

WAKE UP AMERICA

Our country is facing immoral decay,
Where murders now go free,
And harm a child, you hardly pay,
Just a short time and a small fee,

Kids in school, have gone berserk,
Attacking and killing one another,
In all the states, evil lurks,
Decency and compassion they smother,

Liberal judges and teachers are to blame,
At justice and decency they sneer,
They feel no regret and no shame,
And show no cause of fear,

Guns replaced God, in our schools,
They want the flag to also go,
Patriotism and religion, they consider fools,
Bending our country, to an all time low,

People fear terrorists and the bomb,
But they better take a second look,
Our courts and schools cause alarm,
Be aware, and understandably shook,

WAKE UP AMERICA", don't let them win
They're the enemy, we must replace,
They want our country to fall from within,
Our enemies,...... with a domestic face.

By Mickey Deegan

"JUST FOR LETTING HIM"

A darling, little baby boy, not quite a year,
Can bring a smile, a frown... or even bring a tear,
He'll crawl about the house, and then look all around,
Heaven knows what's in his mind, or just where he's bound,

He'll upset you, by getting into everything in sight,
You're always on his path, from morning until night,
But still and all it warms my heart, to follow his devilish glee,
To pick up and put back in place, everything I see,

For I thank Thee God, for giving him hands, so strong and sturdy,
I thank thee too, for giving him legs, that allow him to get dirty,
Thanks too, for giving him good eyes, so that he may see,
Yes! Even though they sometimes look, mischievous as can be,

I say a prayer to you dear God, each time I have to look,
To pick up a pot, a toy a pencil, or a book,
Even though You hear me scold, You know that deep within,
I thank Thee God with all my heart, "JUST FOR LETTING HIM".

By Mickey Deegan

"JUST ONE SMILE"

When the world is dark and dreary and everything seems blue,
It's only what people make it and it can be changed by you,

It doesn't cost a penny and it is really worth your while,
To change the world and make it gay by just one little smile,

You can make a world of laughter with just a smile and a cheer,
It's better than having gloom in the air or the sadness of a tear,

A smile can bring both joy and gladness to all our fellow men,
Brush away the gray skies and make the sun shine again,

And remember it will come back to you, for a smile is merely lent,
And it has such great value but it doesn't cost a cent.

By Mickey Deegan

"KATHLEEN"

Dedicated to my daughter

There was a little baby girl, whose eyes were big and bright,
Who gave to life, love and joy and filled me with delight,
You were so much fun to play with, an answer to a dream
When I was young, my very wish, was to have, my own Kathleen,

You filled my life, as you grew, with a grace, that is so rare,
The sincerity and love, you gave me was far beyond compare,
Now, a young lady, not just a daughter, but a true and lasting friend,
Sometimes, I remember, when things went wrong,
you'd always help them mend,

You've also been, my loyal confidant, which I will always treasure,
What you are in my life, there are no ways to measure,
You grew to be a lovely, girl, who fills me with a pride,
And now you enter a new life, as you become a bride,

You should always have true happiness, a road that's free of care,
All the good things life can offer, may you always have your share,
The best wish, I could wish for you, that's filled with love serene,
That God be as good to you as me, and give you,…. Your own "Kathleen".

By Mickey Deegan

ANN BETH

Dedicated to my daughter

You arrived here on earth, a beauty from the start,
My second little baby girl, a joy that filled my heart,
I wanted the name Ann and Beth was special too,
So I combined both and made an extra special you,

A tiny precious little girl, as good as you could be,
That very special bond was made... between you and me,
I even felt back then, I wish these days would last,
It's now such a luxury, to slip back into the past.

You grew form babyhood, gentle and somewhat shy,
All too fast, those treasured years, seemed to slip right by,
Remember... how you hid behind me, when a stranger said hello,
You'd hold on for dear life and never let me go.

As you grew to womanhood, your gentleness survived,
Your lady-like way, filled me with a pride,
Compassion for others, especially the very old,
Has always been a part of you, stories that are untold.

I'll always treasure, those talks, that went late into the night,
Discussing all life's problems, and trying to make them right,
You are truly a listener, a quality that is so rare,
You're one of the very few, showing that you care,

Another era unfolds and becomes part of your life,
As you enter into matrimony, and become a wife,
May you be blessed with happiness and free from all despair,
All the good and wonderful things, may you always get your share,

If along life's bumpy road, things get a little out of hand,
There is someone always there, who will understand,
And in your life, I hope I'll always have a part,
You see, I'm still carrying you,......... but now you're in my heart.

By Mickey Deegan

EVIL POLITICAL POWER

Dedicated to the liberals

There are so many among us now, a frightening thing,
You'll know who they are, as soon as their voices ring,

There called Liberals, mostly Democrats you see,
They are Anti-American, powerful they want to be,

They are full of hate, for President Trump, because he has a stand,
To help all Americans and again make this country grand,
He said citizenship should be given to legal immigrants after a ten-year stay,
That would certainly be right, they earned it… it wasn't given away,

The liberals want them to vote immediately in three years,
They feel that would give them votes, and silence their fears,

Illegal immigrants should not have the right, to vote a President in,
The liberals want them to vote in just three years, so they can win,

The liberals want the Political Power, they don't care what Americans say,
So, they can have sanctuary states and all their evils their way.

At the union speech, they didn't stand for the anthem or the American Flag,
Just like our enemies now, they too think they can brag,

I hope the real patriotic Americans saw all they have to know,
How the Liberal Anti -Americans, put on their shameful show,

May President Trump forever keep, God by his side,
Americans love their country and display our flag with pride.

By Mickey Deegan

"DESERTED TOYS"

Deafening silence enfolds the house, as I go about the day,
Glancing out to the empty yard, where the children play,
Deserted toys, empty chairs, there stands the silent pool,
How different things appear to be, on this first day of school,

There's the rope swing Timmy made, blowing from the tree,
And Kathleen's carriage, with her doll, seems idle as can be,
Ann Beth s ball is standing still and there's the quiet horn,
I can't help but wonder, how things look so forlorn,

I think of the times, I couldn't wait, for this very day,
Somehow, I didn't really expect, it would be just this way,
There's a little a lump in my throat, how often it was sore,
For all the times I had to yell, over their playful roar,

It's almost too much for me to bear, I really miss them so,
I watch the clock tick away, how it seems so slow,
I hear the bus, they have returned bursting with school news,
Immediately, there in the door, how fast I lost the blues,

They screamed all at once to me, I couldn't hear a word,
Running to and fro, like an uncontrollable herd,
I started yelling once again, as I thought with a smile,
I can't wait till tomorrow, for peace and serenity awhile.

By Mickey Deegan

"AN EMPTY CHRISTMAS"

In a quiet little room, sits an elderly pair,
Although there is a Christmas tree, the house seems so brave,

What is missing, that makes things so sad,
What seems so wrong with this Mom and Dad,

As I glance around the room and try to guess,
I see a sailor's picture, which stands in loneliness,

A picture of their son, who lost his life at sea,
A boy who no more Christmases, will he ever see,

Some people are joyful and celebrate, on this day,
While some people are lonely and in a sad way,

We must remember those, who haven't joy and bliss,
For there's many in this world, that have an empty Christmas.

By Mickey Deegan

"GET UP AND START AGAIN"

When you have fallen on your face, You feel pretty low, what then!
Leave discouragement don't leave a trace, "Get up and start again."

When you tried and things go wrong, So what!
It happened to greater men,
Face the world with a cheerful song,
"get up and start again."

When others will try to discourage you,
And tell you how things have been,
Well, then you know that's your cue
"Get up and start again."

You'll work hard all through the year,
You struggle and say I can,
If you fall don't show a tear,
"Get up and start again."

By Mickey Deegan

"FLAG'S AND RIBBONS"

Down the many highways and the quiet neighborhood street,
The flags are proudly flying and the ribbons tied so neat,

There are yellow bows on cars and trees and fences too,
Giving the same message as the red, white and blue.

A nation that's burdened with a war... united and proudly stands,
Watching over her young and brave, as they serve in foreign lands;

And even though we must lead the world in freedom's fight,
There's always terrible price to pay, when displaying our needed might.

Our nation's greatest loss is that of a life, of a son,
So you see, we lose...... even after the battles are won,

No more Vietnams.... from now we fight, to win.
Destroy the enemy, finish them fast, though so very grim,

So when you notice a yellow ribbon and the red white and blue, you see fly,
You'll know it's a message of love, from each one of us........ to each and every G.I..

By Mickey Deegan

"MY DADDY"

Dedicated to all good Daddies

My daddy, is one who's larger than life, in a pair of little eyes,
And he's always considered no matter what, to be very, very wise,

He's watched what he does, at both work and play, and how he handles defeats,
He's a good loser, when the game is lost and humble when he beats,

He's watched how he treats other people too, especially his very own wife,
A lesson learned, of his kindness and love, his protection of all in her life,

My daddy is strong and unafraid, he's always there, especially if I fall
His arms protect me, he wipes all tears, he's there for each needy call,

My daddy is giving all that he can, but he always wants to give more,
To me and my Mom, he's our hero, one who we will always adore,

I look up to him and I'm so proud, this wonderful man is my dad,
If every kid doesn't have one, just like him...... that's so very, very sad,

By Mickey Deegan

FINAL CHANCE TO SAVE AMERICA

We lost a true American, Scalia from the supreme court,
Now to replace him, a battle definitely must be fought,
You… the republicans is a must that you act.
In the past, you let us down. That certainly is a fact,
You gave Obama everything, cash and all the rest.
To defend America, you didn't act for the people's best.

Now it is crucial you turn down all he will nominate,
To stay in the wrong direction so he can dominate,
Our future is scary, if you turn your backs, on us once more,
Our country must be guided, with justice and fair law,
We voted you in to destroy him and his unjust, un American way.
We hoped you would be loyal Americans and save the day.

Our constitution and laws, have been under attack,
In the past you our congress, showed us the guts you lack,
If you fail this time, to stand up and win this fight,
America's future as we know it will no longer be bright,
We remind you… you're there, to keep America safe and strong,
We the people, hope you'll show the strength to right the wrong.

By Mickey Deegan

"SOMEONE CARES"

Someone cares about,
The things you do and say,
Someone's thoughts are with you,
every night and everyday,

someone hopes and prays,
that all your dreams come true,
someone's always wishing.
They can spend their life with you,

Someone really cares if you're happy or if you're sad,
Someone wants to share with you,
your good times and your bad,

if you're ever lonely, just close your eyes and smile,
someone's there with you,
they've been there all the while,

someone wants you to know,
if you're near or far away,
someone really loves you... and you're in a heart to stay.

By Mickey Deegan

"DANIELLE"

Dedicated To My Granddaughter

God was busy once again, to give this world a lift,
He did His very best, and set a precious gift,
She's such a little angel, so pink and so small,
Just to be near her….. brings happiness to all,

In this dreary world, so filled with strife,
Amidst it all, is this wonderful and holy life.
She makes you feel special, with just a little smile,
You feel once again….. it really is worth while,

You'll be reminded too, just what it's all about,
When you took at her face, with her smile or little pout,
And if you talk to her, she'll search you with her eyes,
You can't help but wonder, so young but so wise,

On Danielle's beautiful face, sits a little turned up nose,

She's perfect, form her head to her toes,
We thank you God for this darling little bundle of charm,
And we promise you,….. to protect her and keep her from all harm.

By Mickey Deegan

"DIDN'T YOU TAKE THE TIME"

If you haven't the time, it takes to love,
People around you and your God above,
What is the purpose... the meaning of life,
Why all the suffering... why all the strife,

Maybe you've accomplished, your work today,
And all the rewards your job has to pay,
You feel fulfilled, though it may be rough,
But ask yourself... is it enough?

Have you showed your loved ones, that you care,
Have you taken a moment... for one little prayer?
Is someone happy... just because of you,
Something you said or something you do,

Your living is honest, commendable your job,
Yet from your loved ones you daily rob,
Affection and time... to you they give,
To keep you nourished and help you to live,

Sad it is, to lose values and sight,
Not knowing the difference of wrong and right,
Not giving love or making a happy home,
And maybe one day... you'll be all alone.

By Mickey Deegan

"A MARINE"

A marine is part of America's best,
A service that's America's pride,
A marine has to pass, every rigid test
Then gallantly... stand by her side.

A marine is trust... with a nation's life,
A pledge he won't betray,
Helping her, in her troubles and strife,
Safe guarding her... night and day.

A marine is honor... on all shores,
Both near and far from home,
For all his history... in both peace and war,
Wherever he may roam.

A marine is proud.. of a job well done,
But takes it all in stride,
Never counting... all the battles won,
While a nation... is busting with pride.

A marine is filled with America's love,
He's everything, for which she stands,
He's also watched by God above,
Home... or in foreign lands.

By Mickey Deegan

"A MARRIAGE PRAYER"

We're taking the step, you and I, we're walking down the aisle,
It's completing our love hopefully forever, that walk… down the carpeted mile,

I know we're thinking both of us and maybe a little afraid,
That we live up to all the promises and commitments to be made,

My prayer, is that you'll always be, loving understanding and kind,
You'll always be the man I love and respect and hope… you'll never change my mind,

That you'll always honor and protect me and be a support by my side,
So I can always look at you, as my friend, my lover, with pride,

If you ever see me lose my smile… and laughter seems to fade,
Be smart enough to know, there's something wrong… with the promises you made,

Like so many others, that we know, their love faded and they fought,
They were in trouble, but didn't care enough and ended up in court,

When love is shattered and goes away it's caused, by betrayal and pain,
Promise me… you'll never let it happen to us and with love… I promise the same.

By Mickey Deegan

FIND A FRIEND

This life is very sad, for animals with no home,
Yet think of all the people lonely, and live alone,

Even all the kids, who like to run and play,
How they would love an animal to be with them every day,

All these people should go to their nearest pound,
How happy they would be, if a adorable animal they found,

Most of them would find a true and gentle friend,
Their loneliness and emptiness soon would all end,

Our four legged friends and folks are happy as can be,
Why don't you go there... and see what you can see.

By Mickey Deegan

"G.I. JOE"

A tired, bent figure came slowly from the hill,
Returning once more, from a never ending drill,
He slowly removes, all his gear and pack,
Thinking to himself, it's good to be back,

He pulls off his boot, so burdened with thought,
He hopes, what he's doing, isn't all for naught,
He lies in bed and thinks with a sigh,
He's pretty darn proud to be a G.I.,

He thinks of his country, the land of the free,
And he knows that he's there,… that it may always be,
He sees the flag, with its red, white and blue,
To keep it flying, he'll do all he can do,

He remembers too, when he was once afraid,
His fear always left him, whenever he prayed,
He thinks of his hometown, his mother and dad,
And how he misses his girl real bad,

Here, he must stay, till the job is done,
He'll know he's helped when the battle is won,
He's a little lonely, like all the rest,
But like them all, he'll do his best,

He'll come home and then, take it all in stride,
But a grateful country, will be busting with pride,
We'll beat any enemy, discourage any foes,
As long as there's guy,… like our "G.I. Joe."

By Mickey Deegan

"ODE TO A PRESIDENT"

A grieving country and tear filled eyes,
Befalls America on this day,
Our flag half-mast, it sadly flies,
For our President has passed away,

Our hearts are heavy, our hopes are dim,
As John F. Kennedy lies in state,
Our love and respect, surrounded him,
Yet, he was killed with a bullet of hate,

He was a man, who held our trust,
His guidance we all felt need,
His enemies, were only the hateful unjust,
As he fought for all races and creed,

Our cry as a nation, we'll carry on his fight,
Now more determined than ever,
God grant us his strength and his might,
So hatred and prejudice we'll server,

We thank God, for having him, though so brief,
He'll be missed in both peace and strife,
Forever, our hearts will hold this grief,
He gave his love, his wisdom,...... his life.

By Mickey Deegan

"A MOTHER'S LOVE"

I've never known, a mother's love, but I know what I would do,
I'd treat her like a royal queen... her whole life through,

I'd want to make her proud of me and be all that I can be,
I'd want to see, her hopes and dreams become reality,

I'd want to share her happy times, but also I'd be there,
Through her trails and sad moments, when things got hard to bear,

I'd take her hand and let her know, she'd never be alone,
I'd be grateful, for the chance to repay all the love, that she has shown,

A Mother's love is beyond compare, it will help you through all strife
If you have it,... ... your possess one of the greatest treasures in life.

By Mickey Deegan

DARLING LITTLE GIRL

Eyes that twinkle, tug at your heart,
Little teeth as white as pearl,
In your life, she has the biggest part,
That darling little girl.

She can smile a smile a certain way,
That sets your heart a whirl,
She brightens up your every day,
That darling little girl.

She's got the cutest turned up nose,
Soft hair that turns in curl,
She puts to shame the prettiest rose,
That darling little girl.

Diamonds, rubies and all other treasures,
All of them, I would gladly hurl,
Away from me, for I own all treasures,
That darling little girl.

By Mickey Deegan

"MISSING SOMEONE"

A little star without the sky,
Can tumble in the dark,
A giant tree can fall and die,
Without it's root and bark.

Picture a beach without the sun,
Cold and oh! so dreary,
Strip a clown of all his fun,
And he'd be sad and weary.

Hide a rose from the rain,
It would fall into the earth,
A fireplace cold, with no flame,
Just what would it be worth?

When one you love, is far away,
Then too, all seems so wrong,
All the nights and everyday,
Are empty and so long.

Someday, I know, again we'll meet,
The sun will shine again,
Life will be so very sweet,
I miss you so……. till then.

By Mickey Deegan

FORSTER

Dedicated to a wonderful dog

I've been here for a while, waiting for a home,
They feed me and like me ... kindness is also shown,
But I long for the love I need, a family to call mine,
People who will keep me and always let me shine.

I have a lot to give, loyalty, protection and love,
I hope to come and get me ... you get a little shove,
I lost my home due to divorce, couldn't be kept
Half starved, cold, all alone, that's how I was left.

I may not be a puppy, I'm about a year old.
I'm too big to adopt, people are sometimes told,
But I'm lovable and adorable, that's what they say,
When you meet me, I'll prove it, in every single way.

My tail is always wagging, my spirt isn't broken,
I'm friendly and lovable to all kinds of folk,
Please come and meet me, I'm patiently waiting here,
To have a life with you and nothing more to fear.

By Mickey Deegan

"CARTER"

Come on, come all, there's a play in town,
Maybe you'll look on, with a bit of a frown,
It's a comedy, that will run for four years,
You'll laugh and laugh, till you're in tears.

Now that Carter, is president – elect,
Washington will change its player and set,
The players weren't always, the best before,
There were a lot of bad actors, and broken law.

The worst actor of all, will play the lead role,
He conquered Ford, and his running mate Dole,
He'll be out on stage, and all the while,
He'll solve all problems, with just one smile.

His philosophy seems, to turn the other cheek,
Remember the earth, will be inherited by the meek,
While our enemies watch, his common sense,
Cheerfully he promised to cut our defense.

Make us weak, while they get stronger,
And our military won't be as big any longer,
He should stick to play boy and all his lust,
Already his play sounds like one big bust.

Oh! He promises too, to give South Korea to the North,
While in his mind... were plunging forth,
He should be where, he can't do no harm,
Back in Georgia...... on his peanut farm.

By Mickey Deegan

"SYMBOLS OF LIFE"

Like words upon paper, this life of mine,
Some........... written long ago,
Looking closely at each, faded line,
A tale,... .... with purpose to show.

A crossed (T), could be a symbol of regret, Never to be undone,
Something that may be, hard to forget,
Like a victory, that wasn't won.

Or a dot over an (i), cannot be returned, Once it's put in place,
Maybe all too late, it was learned,
Like a bet... ...and losing a race.

Some other letters, written with care, Fancy and real wide,
Could mean when skies, were sunny and fair,
Written,..... there with pride.

Like words on paper, a life is made,
The good, the bad, ...all there,
Someday... ...it too will also fade.
Like words,..... that were written there.

By Mickey Deegan

"I REMEMBER"

I think of you, day by day,
Thoughts of you fill my head,
I remember you so, in every way,
As I recall all the things you said,

I remember too, when I see the sun,
The casual way you smile,
Especially at night, when day is done,
In the darkness, you linger awhile,

I seem a little lost in the rain,
It never seemed dreary before,
We'd laughing go down the lane,
It isn't that way, anymore,

I remember all things, we used to do,
I was happy just to pretend,
It would last forever, being with you,
I've always known someday, it would end,

You're like a bird, that must be free,
You'll travel your road alone,
You stopped for awhile and noticed me,
Then went on to leisurely roam,

How could you know, you took my heart,
I tried telling you, but you didn't hear,
In my life, you became the biggest part,
Your happiness is all, I held dear,

Although you travel, so independently,
And maybe you really don't care,

Look around you and try to see,
We're together in thought and prayer,

I remember the stranger, who happened by,
And stole my heart, silently away,
I fell in love, without reasoning why,
And loved you more, each day,

As life brings you, to your own fate,
When all your dreams, come true,
Will you sometimes, stop and hesitate,
And think of someone, who remembers you

By Mickey Deegan

"AMERICA...THE WAY IT USED TO BE"

America was always laughter and fun,
And always patriotism, held high,
Enjoying our freedom and victories won,
From the battles, long gone by,

People neighborly and do communicate,
In the country and land they share,
By appearance alone, they can relate,
As in language, and what they wear,

Strangers, have come with strange tongue and dress,
With no intentions, to change their way,
Our lands and benefits, they immediately possess,
As they crowd into the U.S.A.,

Hundreds of different languages are spoke,
Foreign dress, is constantly worn,
Not acting like Americans, but to provoke,
A country is that being torn,

Politicians do nothing to correct this divide,
If we're not united, we will fall,
Others who came, stood by America's side,
As Americans.... they stood proud and tall,

We want back our language and our country,
Our traditions will not be shaken,
By these intruders, who came by sea,
And causes us a great awaken,

We'll not allow them to pose a threat,
To this great land of liberty,

Our style and values they can't accept
And Americans... for all to see,

We love our country, far and wide
Great people have come to our shores,
To protect our life, men have died,
To keep our values and our laws,

They have a choice, to leave or stay,
To be Americans, like you and me,
To pledge their loyalty to the U.S.A,
We want America.... the way it used to be.

By Mickey Deegan

"IF TODAY WAS MY VERY LAST"

If you knew today, was my last,
You would probably be so kind,
The day would be treasured, as the past,
Wonderful memories, would come to mind.

If you love me, it would surely show,
You wouldn't keep it, ...so safe hid,
Now you would really want me to know,
And say things, ... your never did,

You would want me, to spend a day serene,
Everything....you would probably do,
You would want to fulfill my every dream,
Wishing the hours, ...weren't too few.

But now I 'm here, and hope to be,
Around for quite a while,
Be and do all those things for me,
Turning my tears... into a smile.

I'm thankful today is not my very last,
And when all is said and done,
Your love should always be steadfast
Keeping me as your special one.

By Mickey Deegan

HAPPY BIRTHDAY TIMMY

Dedicated to my Son

Today is my son's birthday, I feel so very low,
You see, I lost him some time ago.

He used to fill my heart, with laughter and cheer,
I wish every day, that he was still here.

Sometimes he would make me mad and we would fight
But that would soon pass, much to my delight,

He became a marine, which he always wanted to be,
He made our country proud, as proud as he made me.

I know now he's with God, he was very loyal to him.
In his heart, he carried that love very deep within.

When my time comes, I hope I'll see him up above,
So I can still show him my everlasting love,

I hope he can see me and also that he can hear,
All the others that miss him, and will always hold him dear.

By Mickey Deegan

"LOST FRIEND"

I have so many blessings God, I count them in my mind,
I understand how good you are to me and how very kind,

Forgive me God for being blue my heart weary and sad,
I never thought it possible, to feel so very bad,

I lost my friend you see, he was indeed the very best,
Remember God... you took him home and gave him peaceful rest,

I accept your will but down deep inside, my heart is filled with
pain,
Tearfully I look for him... knowing it be in vain,

My heart gets a little joy my mind a little ease,
If I know he's with you,... ... Oh! How I ask it please,

My eyes lift up to him dear God and I know he hears what I say,
He hears me pray that I be good, so I may see him again one day.

By Mickey Deegan

"LIFE OF AN AGENT"

A typical day in our office, is as busy as can be,
There's agents going to and from, with plenty of houses to see,
Phones are ringing off the hook, buyers looking for a steal,
If you can get, a meeting of the minds, you can get a deal,

But that is far from each owner has a … …palace,
If you give a true appraisal, you are treated with such malice,
They want a price, though unreal, they're filled with pure greed,
They think their houses is made of gold… that tiny little deed,

Then you get the buyer, who wants it all and the best,
Neighborhood and condition, including all the rest,
Must have three bedrooms, full basement and garage,
And don't forget, all the rooms must be very, very large,

Then the best part comes, you ask them what they can spend,
The only way they can buy… is with a friendly little lend,
They tell you the highest they can go, is a whooping three twenty,
But don't forget, for that price, they want it all and plenty,

Then you take your magic wand and wave it with a sigh,
A good agent, certainly would never, never say die,
You try to keep your sense of humor, and handle it with a smile,
Because you will get buyers and sellers that are sane… every once in awhile.

By Mickey Deegan

"MERRY CHRISTMAS MOM AND DAD"

Merry Christmas Mom and Dad is what a sailor wrote,
While people are enjoying Christmas he's somewhere on a boat,

Merry Christmas, Merry Christmas goes over in their minds,
That means all the world to them, just those two little lines,

Merry Christmas Mom and Dad is the message from their boy,
That's all they needed to bring them, both happiness and joy,

And a Merry Christmas to you my son, they both tearfully said,
As they picked up the letter once more and repeated the words it read,

How wonderful it is, when you are not sad,
And all because of one little line "Merry Christmas Mom and Dad"

By Mickey Deegan

"OPEN LETTER TO PRESIDENT NIXON"

Mr. Nixon we're with you, just as before,
When you settled the crisis of the Vietnam war,
With faith we anxiously await the proof,
That beyond all doubt, you told the truth,

The Watergate scandal.... may be wrong,
But the democrats aren't perfect... we've known all along,
So your aids were caught, because of the bug,
Now the democrats are God, Jury and Judge,

Yet Ellsberg acquitted, the thief of pentagon papers,
The law turned liberal, to his criminal capers,
You own the election, with a vote so great,
You didn't need help, from things like Watergate,

The people are with you and we're sick and tired,
How your enemies now, are trying to get you fired,
They're crying impeachment, to get rid of you,
Because they say... you really knew,

If you did, we'll not reverse our stand,
You're still the best President for this land,
Let those without guilt, cast the first stone,
You'll soon find out, you're far from alone,

You'd be surrounded by Democrats, as one by one,
If the truth were known, for the things they've done,
If put to the people... let us decide,
You still would win, with the greatest landslide,

So were behind you, we just want you to know,
We can't wait till the end, of the Watergate show.

By Mickey Deegan

"KNOW THYSELF"

Sometimes we find, we criticize a little bit too much,
Maybe a little unaware of the feelings that we crush,
Sometimes we say a harsh word, that we never really meant,
In someone's ego, to be sure we really put a dent.

Would you be the cause for a tear, so sadly shed,
Think of it a minute... was it something that you said,
Would you deliberately change a smile to a saddened face,
Because of a snicker, or a laugh that was out of place.

It really is so easy to spread sugar and spice,
It's also very easy to like someone who is nice,
But it takes a lot of work and more practice to be mean,
It's really unhappiness doing its work and plotting every scheme.

"Know Thyself" and weigh your words as if they were of gold,
Give generously if they're good, but stingily if they're bold,
Be merciful of your fellow men, whoever they may be,
Remember... "I do unto you, what I would want you to do unto me."

By Mickey Deegan

"LIFE'S PUZZLED DAYS"

Sometimes people always shout,
Or they even cry
Some of them even pout
Not knowing the reasons why.

People should change for their own sake
And put some smiles back on their face.
Their problems shouldn't overtake,
And be in a nice and happy place.

Even going through things so sad
They should stand strong and tall
Remember even though things are bad.
It's happened to one and all.

Things can change, to a better day
Although now, they seem so bleak.
Knowing yourself in a better way
If your strong or if your weak.

Remember... you're not all alone
There's someone you cannot see,
Someday you'll be fully shown,
Someone's helping both you and me.

By Mickey Deegan

"KING"

Went to get a puppy, long ago one day,
Saw a little furry shepherd, all ready to play,
Picked him up and held him tight, in a little hug,
He licked my cheek and settled in a comfy snug.

It was love at first sight, I couldn't let him go,
Looking at that adorable face, it was easy to know,
I didn't have to look further, he was coming home with me,
He too like all of us..., was as happy as can be.

"King" is now eleven years old, worth his weight in gold,
He's still elegantly handsome, though starting to get old,
He's so important in my life, my loyal and true friend,
Just him being there..., helps my trouble mend.

I can't picture me, without him close to share,
All the crosses in my life, that I have to bear,
I thank God for this gift, my furry everything,
He's truly deserving of his name..., my faithful and loyal "King."

By Mickey Deegan

"CHALLENGING GAME CALLED LIFE"

Sometimes we take life for granted good times comfort and such,
Sometimes we are so unaware, we may have a bit too much,
It's not until, we have to struggle, we find what life is all about,
It's having to face uncertainly, … and a future filled with doubt.

Then we get to know ourselves and the strength we've got inside,
Accepting life and its' knocks and taking it in stride,
We can find out then if we can walk real tall,
Or if we buckle and come out bent and small.

We'll ask for courage, from way up high, we really need a loan,
Then somehow things look better…. when we know we're not alone,
We surprise ourselves, it's good to know, we're better than we thought,
We're facing up to the war of life and our battles are well fought

Things can look so very bad, days filled with dark and gloom,
But we believe; things will change,… …the sun will shine real soon,
And we're just a little better for the way we handled strife,
And now we've played a bigger part….. in the challenging game called life.

By Mickey Deegan

"YOU PASSED BY"

Dedicated to Mgr. Joseph Parks

You passed by, along life's hard road,
And stretched out your hand,
You lifted the burden and lessened the load,
Always ready to understand.

You passed by, when despair was near,
With words your only tool,
The mountain of trouble seemed to disappear,
I was easily a fool.

You passed by and showed me too,
How humble once can be,
Someone with great esteem as you,
Befriend one like me.

You passed by and spent awhile,
You have a special way,
To change a frown to a smile,
And brighten up a day.

You passed by and made a life,
Richer because your there,
You helped see through trouble and strife,
And lessen every... anxious care.

You passed by on life's busy street,
The wrong or the right I'll do,
Where I'll go... or who I'll meet,
I'm better... for knowing you.

By Mickey Deegan

"LITTLE THINGS"

It's the little things you do for me, that makes me love you so,
The kindness of your heart and the way you come and go,

It's the smile upon your face you carry everywhere,
Through each dreary moment and through every anxious care,

It's the way you understand, all the little things I do,
And the way you try to help me make all my dreams come true,

Though you think they go unnoticed, I really see them all,
Your always there to answer my every needy call,

And though you think the things you do, really don't amount,
It's the little things you do for me,

THE THINGS THAT REALLY COUNT!!!!!

By Mickey Deegan

"OUR NORTH STAR"

Dedicated to Col. Oliver North

The contra hearings are the talk everywhere.
Emotions are running high,
Ollie North did more than to catch him life,

Americans like him, make congress look sick,
With their attitudes, holier than thou,
They're trying to use every dirty trick.
But the people.... have joined in now,

We're tried patriotism, being put on trail,
With honor and integrity a sin,
Congress seems, completely senile,
We know Ollie, will surely win,

They use such words as impeach and indict,
Against Americans,.... that are great,
We'll jump in and join the fight,
And stop the communist hate,

We voted them in; we'll vote them out,
Congress is a national disgrace,
Let's show them now without a doubt,
They have stepped, way out of place,

Ollie kicked some butt on TV,
As they went on and on, to grill,
Single-handed, for the world to see,
He took, the congressional hill,

We're proud of Olli, for what he's done,

He's captured America's heart,
When this congressional battle is finally won,
We'd like him again to start,

To stand by the President and America's side,
We need him now, more than ever.
He's our hero and we're filled with pride,
Men like him,…. a legacy lives on forever.

By Mickey Deegan

"LOVED AND LOST"

I had 5 German sheperds, loved each one,
Each and every one of them was such great fun,
Each was so smart, they understood and obeyed
I loved them as puppies and hopelessly saw them old and fade.

I owned them separately, they lived till they grew old,
Each and every one was worth their weight in gold,
I am still sad for Shep, Regal, Ranger, Foxy and King,
They will always be in my heart, they were my everything.

I now have Scout, the first I got from the pound,
He makes me happy too, just to be around.
It's because of the money, I couldn't get a Pedigree,
He's three quarters Sheperd and Doberman you see.

I love him too, just like all the rest,
To have an animal by your side, certainly is the best.
If again I lost my 13 year old Scout, who I truly love,
Please God, let me see them all, when we meet with you above.

By Mickey Deegan

"FROM A DEAD MARINE"

Dedicated to Pfc. Michael A. McDermott 11150175

I was a marine, who fought in Korea and was killed in 1952,
I shed my blood for my country, and gave my life for you,
The greatest pain was leaving my loved ones, never to return to the U.S.A,.
When life was good and free, I remember the American way.

But now I feel sad, angry and very much betrayed.
The country I loved and died for let decency and justice fade
A little kid can't mention God's name in school,
And most of the seats in your congress, are filled with political fools.

You took a guy like Ollie North, a patriot and pinned him to the wall,
If you could see yourselves, from where I am, You look so very, very small,
And now you want to add a new language, that just don't belong,
You seem to have lost all your fight, for righting all the wrong.

And now let your flag be burned, by any radical foe,
The flag I and so many died for, so it should wave and forever show,
Your country is being threatened, the home of the free and the brave,
The good and decent people are angry and filled with unheeded rage.

I'm glad I lived in America, when to be one filled you with a pride,
All I can do now for you is pray... and hope God stays by your side.

By Mickey Deegan

"MY FRIEND, THE PRESIDENT"

I saw you often, in many a way,
Television, papers and such,
I was looking toward that one day,
Your great hand, sometime I'd touch,

I loved you so, with great esteem,
So strong, fair and unafraid,
You had for your country, the greatest dream,
Your hopes to fulfill…….. I prayed.

And now Mr. Kennedy, you lie in state,
My heart and my spirits are broke,
Without you, I'm afraid, of what's ahead,
Me… and a lot of folk,

I know you hear, Mr. Kennedy, I'll try not to cry,
Why this happened, nobody can tell me why.
The man who shot you I shouldn't hate, I'll do my best,
But from his hand you met your fate and now you lay in rest.

To me, you were one swell guy,
I know God must think so too,
I bet your job, is still real high,
In heaven, where there's lots to do,

Mr. Kennedy, forgive the tears you see,
I'll go now and thanks again,
For being President of my country and me
And for helping all your fellowmen.

By Mickey Deegan

"GOD NEEDED AN ANGEL"

Our little boy went off to bed one fair and starry night,
The moon was out and the stars were shining in all their glory and might,

Our little boy was always good, fair, honest and true,
All little things, he saw undone, he would always do,

Upon his face, he always wore a gentle little smile,
When he was near, he'd cheer you and make life worthwhile,

As morning came, I heard no sound, the morning was growing old,
Silently, I went up the stairs, and in his room I stole,

Everything was very still, I could not hear a sound,
For our little, boy has passed away… and a better world he found.

We were once sad and did not understand why this had to be,
But let me try to tell you…, the way God had told it to me.

"I have a lot of angels who are in heaven here with me,
They are never lonely, they're as happy as can be,

There was one little cloud, vacant and no one for this place,
We had to select somebody kind and with a gentle face,

My angels have no sadness, they know nothing else but joy,
And out of all my earthly creatures I have chosen your little boy."

By Mickey Deegan

"NO DARE CALL IT TREASON"

The number is, just a very few,
But their noise your sure to hear,
They're disrespectful and loud in all they do,
Their hope... to spread violence and fear.

They disregard both country and flag,
They're a national disgrace,
For all their mis-deeds they all brag,
Slapping old glory in the face.

There is punishment that should be paid,
By this ignorant and noisy group,
But even though every attempt is made,
They escape, in some political loop.

There are some politicians who disregard,
The injustices inflicted on this land,
All arguments morally right... are barred,
The people suffer at their treasonous hand.

Even our courts fail... to interrupt,
And stop the crimes that are being done,
Because some of the judges are so corrupt,
Or out of fear the criminals, have won,

In spite of all this... we Americans are proud,
When the stars and stripes go by,
With national anthem our voices grow loud,
And heads are up real high.

We'll right our wrongs, it won't be in one day,
And we'll do it all... within reason,
We'll rid our country of the sick decay,
That now... "None dare call it treason."

By Mickey Deegan

"THE DOCTOR"

The doctor is someone, who scurries around,
He's always here and there,
Every minute of everyday, he's bound,
To have someone in his care,

Some are serious and some are funny,
Sometimes you'll find one crank,
Yet, they can make a day real sunny,
By being cautious kind and frank,

One you'll go to feeling so sick.
Can talk to you for a while,
His sincerity and kindness did the trick,
As you leave with a brand new smile,

Yet one can scare you, half to death
With a needle, sharp and thin,
You feel you're drawing your latest breath,
Your confidence, he fails to win,

There are all sorts of doctors, short and tall,
Serious, funny and nice,
Each one of them answering the call,
For their needed and learned advice,

There's the doctor who puts you at ease right away,
We trust, he'll make us well,
We listen to everything he has to say,
We consider him just swell,

Especially the one who remembers our name,
He's knows our every complaint,

He's always nice and always the same,
To us, he's a living saint,

Of course there are doctors who never grin,
These kinds I just can't see,
After examining you, they'll give you aspirin,
And charge you an enormous fee,

We trust the doctor with our very life,
He has patience and kindness it's true,
He helps us, through our everyday strife,
Without him....... What would we do??

By Mickey Deegan

MY SISTER NANCY

It's Thanksgiving Day, your physically hot here, but deep within my heart,
You have and always will have the greatest part.

I miss you so, it's hard for me, to get through any day,
To be with you forever, I certainly pray.

I hope you're with all loved ones, like Freddy, Timmy and Marie,
Then I know you're happy and many more I pray you see.

Wait for me Nancy, when I too will leave this life,
Hopefully leaving behind all the sadness and strife.

I will miss some people, but be with the one since my birth,
Proud to call my sister and treasure her love and her worth.

By Mickey Deegan

WHAT PRICE MY LOVE

What price my love, I must pay,
For the love, I have for you
It grows in me, with each new day,
In my thoughts, with each task I do.

But there's only one very small part,
Of all of me that's free,
To love you dear, that's my heart,
Where your ever close to me.

It was too late, from the very start,
That day, when our eyes had met,
In someone's life I had a part,
Like a stage that's already been set.

A love within me burns real deep,
In a world that is my own,
It taught me well, how to weep,
And when with people...... to feel alone.

I know well too how to silently grieve,
As life greets me day by day,
To forget you, is when I'll cease to breath,
For loving you......this price I must pay.

By Mickey Deegan

"THE YANKEES"

Dedicated to Yankees in 2004

The World Series again came around this year,
As everyone was set, with a roar and a cheer,

The Red Sox played well, the Yankees too,
The fans took their place to be loyal and true,

The Red Sox came through with their first wins,
Then they walked around with ironical grins,

Then the Yankees came and evened the score,
And made lungs exhausted, with appreciate roar,

The Red Sox came up and again and won,
But this didn't mean the Yankees were done,

The last game was played the Red Sox on top,
But the dear fighting Yankees, just wouldn't stop,

Alas, the Red Sox, won the game,
Like in the past, they tried the same,

We feel real bad, we're disappointed a lot,
All the Red Sox fans have us on a spot,

But we are assured, the Yankees did their best,
Now they return home to the East and the West,

They laugh at our slogan, with a Red Sox sneer,
But nuts to them all... "Wait Till Next Year"

By Mickey Deegan

"TRUE FRIENDSHIP"

We have all sorts of friends,
as I guess you already know,
Some will remain with us,
the rest will come and go,

It's enough to have but one friend,
who will stay with us through the years,
One who will take part in our happiness,
and share in all our tears,

Now, for some reason you sit alone,
friends have left you there,
And there He'll be your true loyal friend,
He's with you everywhere,

You'll feel a little downhearted,
when the sunshine leaves the day,
But He'll be there to comfort you,
in a kind and friendly way,

Then you'll know your true friend,
He'll shine from all the rest,
He's your God and your friend
He's there above the rest.

By Mickey Deegan

"THE WINDOW"

A little girl, stood so silently,
Beside a window sill,
Gazing out at leaves and tree,
Everything was still,
Each day she dreamt, at that place,
Through the window pane,
A-round, sad-eyed-little face,
Looked back at her in vain.

Someday she'll grow up,... wait and see,
Unhappiness will fade,
All her dreams...,will really be,
Her plans have all been laid.
Everynight, she sees her favorite star,
She whispers a little prayer,
It twinkles back... from so very far,
At the little figure there.

There is no Mommy or Daddy to love,
She thought this, to be wrong,
But her fate was planned from above,
It wouldn't be..., for long,
Someday, somewhere there's a little boy,
They'll grow up and they'll meet,
He'll fill her life with song and joy,
Her dreams will be complete.

He'll protect her through the darkest night,
He'll quiet all her fear,
Her little star that shines so bright,
Promised... he'll be there,
No more will she ever be afraid,

He will understand,
This is the prayer, that she has prayed,
He'll gently take her hand.

She'll be his queen and forever reign,
On the throne of love,
Then she'll know to her...,he finally came,
It was promised form above,
Now in the window she can plainly see,
A tiny, little smile,
As she thinks how wonderful life will be,
In just... a little while.

By Mickey Deegan

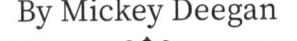

"SOMETHING TO REMEMBER"

Once the flowers bloomed and all the skies were blue,
That's when I was happy, happy because of you,

We used to meet when school was over and sit under our favorite tree,
All cares and worries were washed away, by the love you had for me,

The birds would sing and the perfumed air blew all joys our way,
I was by your side,……. and that's where I longed to stay,

But now as I return and stand on the spot, where all our joys were found,
And watch the dead leaves fall from the trees, which make the only sound.

My cheeks are wet with tears and my heart is filled with sorrow,
As I remember all the yesterdays and think of the empty tomorrow,

I sit alone on the cold, dead grass, which once was covered with clover,
Half wondering, half believing, that happiness and love are over,

A I stand here and realize, you'll never come back to me,
I see our names carved deep in our favorite apple tree,

I have something to remember and in my heart, it will forever stay,
I'll comeback to my memories tomorrow, …. I'll come back everyday.

By Mickey Deegan

"MY SISTER, MY BESTFRIEND"

Even though this world is evil and very bad.
I had someone to turn to, when I was troubled or sad.

She was my sister Nancy, who has now gone home to rest.
She was kind, thoughtful, considerate and to me the very best.

Her life was tough, foster homes and people who were mean,
But together she and I, made a true and loyal team.

She'll stay a part of me, deep within my heart,
My spirits are broke, I feel so sad, but when I depart.

I pray to see her, Timmy and Freddy a joyous reunion for all.
Now I wait and pray for strength, till I too get God's call.

By Mickey Deegan

"SALVATION"

How very mistaken, we sometimes are,
Believing in fantasies or a far away star,
We cling to an idea, that won't materialize,
Though we think, at the time, we were very wise,

For some it's memory, they'll devote their life,
In return, they get nothing, but sorrow and strife,
For others, to someone they're eternally bound,
Only to be hurt and many times let down,

How many of us, are on the wrong track,
And it's a bumpy road and a long way back,
With a false salvation, you strive ahead,
Believing and hoping, till we're dead,

You've got to know the answer is above,
Filled with glory and divine love,
This you must try to obtain,
All the rest is worthless and in vain,

You must realize form the day of your birth,
How important you are and your worth,
No riches or gold could ever compare,
To the human soul, that is so rare,

Live your life, with self-esteem,
Soon you'll conquer your every dream,
Your very important, on this sod,
Remember always, … …you're a child of God.

By Mickey Deegan

LIN

Dedicated to Kenny's daughter

A beautiful flower, that graced the world,
A girl called Lin,......my little girl,
She budded in youth, a beauty so rare,
All who knew her.....just had to care.

And though so young, and filled with love,
God has beckoned.....to her from above,
It was his will, to call her home,
Leaving me heartbroken, and feeling alone.

Now I try to lean, on faith that's shook,
Remembering bitterly.....all that he took,
My heart is heavy with unendurable weight,
Trying so hard, to accept this fate.

Maybe I'll try to think of her awhile,
There in heaven, with a lasting smile,
All pain and suffering for her..... no more,
To joy and happiness, He has opened the door.

Help me God, to know and accept at last,
All earthly sufferings for her past,
Help me with.....my own torment and pain,
When my courage and faith seem to wane.

And let her courage, now by my guide,
She's my very own angel, with whom I confide,
I know she'll lead me, so I don't go astray,
If I stumble or falter, along the way.

Help me to believe, with all my heart,
When the day finally comes, for me to depart,
All my sufferings too, will forever cease,
We'll be together again, in everlasting peace.

By Mickey Deegan

"THE MOON"

1ˢᵗ poem

The moon is looking sad tonight,
And down below, are all bright lights,

Here I am, looking form a windowsill,
Looking at the moon that stands so still,

His little round face, looks as sad as mine,
Although it looks so very kind,

And even though the moon looks bright,
It's very sad tonight.

By Mickey Deegan

"NANCY"

Nancy, is a beautiful name,

Her love and sweetness is the same,

This name, belongs to a special girl,

She has brown hair, with lots of curl,

In all the world, I think she's the best,

Yes! She's my sister, as you can guess.

By Mickey Deegan

"THEY NEED US"

There are dogs and cats, and animals of every kind.
Some are cared for, but others you will find,

Are treated very badly; half-starved and get abuse,
Beaten and chained and never turned loose.

They are owned by evil people who don't care,
The cruelty and pain they make their animals bear.

If they don't get caught and sent to jail,
'Cause too many of us don't see and many of us fail

To pay attention all around us, on this cruelty and hate.
These animals don't deserve to have such fate.

Let's join and become one, do what we have to do.
They are sad and waiting for help from me and you.

By Mickey Deegan

"THE EVIL WORLD"

All this world, is in trouble from bad and evil men,
Things have changed... nothing is the way had been.

In every country, people are being killed with bullets and with fire,
It seems the bad are winning, killing all who we admire.

I wonder where is God, He could stop all the evil ways,
Our time is running out, but we still have many days.

To see death of good people, and Christians being beheaded.
All this life is horrible and the future is being dreaded.

God has come and help us all, who will pray.
He can do it all if we listen to what he'll say.

Now the time has come to help people who will call,
For help, before it's too late and all of us will fall.

By Mickey Deegan

"OLD GLORY"

There are many who live in strife,
In so many countries where there is no value on life,
Their freedom is gone... it was taken away,
By the Communists who came, and invaded one day,

They took over their country, rules their land,
It was hard to accept, and harder to understand,
They no longer lived free, and could worship no more,
In their synagogues or church now...behind a closed door,

There's still one country, powerful and strong,
Fighting for freedom and their fight is long,
It's America... that believes in an individual's right,
They fought many years, by day and by night,

To break the chains, around a man's body and sod,
To return his freedom... and worship his God,
How people cheered... and some would cry,
When gratefully the stars and stripes arrive,

It cost many lives... some of America's best,
They believed in a cause, now they lay at rest,
Old Glory is deeply loved, for what it has done,
The battles fought for freedom, and bravely won,

The flag that represents men... with a common cause,
To live in peace and end all wars,
We Americans shall stand and pledge real loud,
To the red, white and blue which we're so proud,

The job's not finished... and many more may die,
To keep Old Glory free and flying high,

We are a nation that's free...... a nation with pride,
And we will win... ...With God on our side.

By Mickey Deegan

"THAT SPECIAL SOMEONE"

I write this poem for everyone, not just for me.
A broken heart is hard to handle. As we all can see.

There is someone gone out of our life, missed so very much.
No longer to laugh and cry with them, or feel their loving touch.

I try to put on a brave face and act so very norm.
No once can really guess how sad I am and very forlorn.

Life goes on for all of us; prayer does help us through.
We go to work; eat and sleep and do all that others do.

We look toward heaven and hope our loved one is there,
And know how much they're missed and how we'll always care.

We have to face reality and face all, after it is said and done.
There is no cure for getting over missing. "that special someone".

By Mickey Deegan

"911"

Ten years, have passed, but only some things remain,
For the victims' families and the lasting pain,

The stars and stripes, that proudly flew,
Now... if you look around they seem so few,

Our military's still fighting and standing real proud,
Their voices head shouting, strong and loud,

We'll fight till victory and our job is done,
We want to go home, after we've won,

This country they say, is in a great divide,
Not all the people, are on America's side,

The liberal Democrats, seem to be our foe,
All they say and do, is a treasonous show,

May God look down on us today,
So sadly changed... is the U.S.A.,

Our heroes answered, our country's call,
With God's help, we'll conquer them all.

By Mickey Deegan

TO MY LOVED ONES

I miss all of you, please hear what I say,
How much I love you, telling you every day,

It's hard for me being here, without all of you,
Not seeing you, is hard in everything I do.

I pray for you all, you're always in my heart,
You'll always be to me, the very biggest part,

These words of love, I hope you're able to see,
When we're together again, how happy we'll all be.
I miss all of you, please hear what I say,
How much I love you, telling you every day,

It's hard for me being here, without all of you,
Not seeing you, is hard in everything I do.

I pray for you all, you're always in my heart,
You'll always be to me, the very biggest part,

These words of love, I hope you're able to see,
When we're together again, how happy we'll all be.

By Mickey Deegan

"OBAMA FOUR MORE YEARS"

The election is now over, all is said and done,
How very sad for me and my country that he won.
I prayed and prayed but God didn't hear,
He didn't seem to listen, what I and my country fear.

Obama is our enemy, he's our enemies' true friend,
The insults and ignorance to our allies he can't mend,...
The economy and unemployment is the worst in our history,
How all those people voted for him, certainly is a mystery.

His hands are in all that dirty, like fast and furious,
How he gets away with all he does, certainly makes me curious.
Who knows where he came from, just where was he born,
Having him elected again, makes us so forlorn.

He's very secretive about his past, college and people he denies,
To be his friends, but we know how he constantly lies.
He would like to rid all religions from this Christian sod,
He's arrogant and bold right up to the face of God.

I think God has other plans, He always backs the U.S.A.
He'll wait and watch and listen for that special day.
When all the people learn, and follow Him to teach,
How we can rid our country of evil, the word is called IMPEACH.

By Mickey Deegan

KEEPING OUR BELIEF

This world has gotten so evil and bad.
Looking and listening about it, makes me sad.

Even some families don't get along,
And countries attack others, which is very wrong.

The terrorists fight and kill, in the name of their god.
To understand and believe this, is so very hard.

Good people are kind and have a different belief:
Give kindness and help to others and to their pain—relief.

We'll fight when we have to, defend all that's good.
Our God knows we're doing all that we should.

We believe in peace and freedom for everyone.
We pray God watches and protects us till it's done.

The terrorists want all of us to believe like them.
We'll keep our Religion.....and to them "Amen".

By Mickey Deegan

SCOUT AND STRUT

The pound is such a noisy place,
And so very, very sad,
To see all those sad eyes and face,
And the smell is even bad.

Walking through, I could hardly see,
All those abandoned creatures,
Barking and jumping, looking at me,
Hoping they had the desirable features.

There he lay, his eyes looking up,
He certainly looked his best,
A black and white shepard mixed pup,
More quiet than the rest.

I picked him and took him home,
Scout is now his name,
But so many times he's left alone,
I know, and that is a shame.

Now he's found a friend, real true,
They run to and fro,
His name is Strut he's handsome too,
Their feelings and caring show.

Strut has become important in his life,
He can't wait 'til visiting day,
For them both, it releases all strife,
In a wonderful, and brotherly way.

Strut also came from the pound,
The very same awful place,
They both were spared and were found,
Now to live... in life's rat race.

By Mickey Deegan

"YOUR SIXTEENTH BIRTHDAY"

Dedicated to Timmy Deegan

Today you start, your sixteenth year,
I look back to memories, With joy and a tear,
How fast the years, Since that October morn,
When then to me.........my son was born.

I look back at that little round smiling face,
In my mind.....All those years I trace,
Your first steps....That first little toy gun,
Constantly to guide you, I would always run.

The toy soldiers.......You looked at no more,
The swiftness of time, has closed a door,
Your first day of school, even though you tried
To be ever so brave, You cried and cried,

Your little hurts, your little fears,
Always I kissed away, all your tears,
Now it seems, like a whole new world,
Your interest in cars and maybe a girl,

The hours we shared, Seem so very few,
I worry and worry, Like all mothers do,
Sometimes, I yell, we seem so far apart,
But you're still my little boy, deep in my heart,

The generation gap, is what they call it today,
We have our differences, In some small way,
The memories I look at.... With some tears,
Are for the times.... Of the gone by years,

The memories I look at... With such joy,
Are the ones that were spent.... With that little boy.

By Mickey Deegan

TO THE LIBERALS

Just because, they disagree with everything we say,
They seem to hate America, in every single way.
Never before has an election, burst with such debate,
Not only disagreement in talk, but there's violence and hate.

Then try to silence us, with fire and breaking into stores,
They're inhuman and want to start, all these hometown wars,
They also burn our great and respected American flag.
They stomp on it and then they take it out to drag.

Can you imagine… if their side had won,
What it would be in the white house after all they had done,
She's a liar, a cheat, and a fraud who should be in jail
He's an impeached president, who really did fail.

Thank God who intervened and saved us once again.
The horrible lost. Imagine how it would have been,
Now their crybabies, cowards and evil cause they lost.
We'll continue to defeat them at any cost.

Trump is good, he'll make America great.
God is on our side, He's protecting our fate,
We have many enemies far and off shire,
But now here at home, were getting many more.

By Mickey Deegan

"OUR FLAG"

Looking out the window, I glanced at our flag.
It hardly was moving and almost seemed to sag,

A slight wind came and it went into a gentle sway
It almost seems like it was sad, Acting in a strange way.

Then I thought, Could it know about its country's woe,
About our enemies and all our domestic foe.

"Our flag" may feel like I do, heart broken for the U.S.A.
Praying to God, things will change if only it could say.

I can't wait for our country to rally, Always being best.
Keeping our friends and allies and defeating all the rest.

We'll get our country back, For all the world to see,
Everyone will be better off, And be as happy as me.

Then again I'll look out to see, Our wonderful flag,
Blowing on its flag pole and never, never, sag,

So many have fought and died for that red, white and blue,
We will always show you "our flag"…………How much we love you.

By Mickey Deegan

THE SPC MARKETING COMPANY

Dedicated to Steve Flanagan

There are so many pages to line up for a book.
Sometimes there is a deadline and everyone's fast and shook.
Pages must be in order and put in perfect count.
The printer is going to turn out a large amount.

There has to be holes made, by machine they are applied.
Some books are thin and some are very, very wide.
The covers are the topper, good color, and some even shine.
That's why the SPC printers are known to be so fine.

Steve is the owner and boss – man to the rest.
His company is known to be one of the very best.
There's Brian, Judy and Ted adding their talents and their art.
For a little over two years, I too was part.

Now things have come to a close; I blame Barack.
May be when he's gone....we can all come back

By Mickey Deegan

THE EMPTY STOCKING

Christmas time is here again, with all the presents and cheer.
Lots of people shopping for gifts for people they hold dear.
Christmas carols fill the air; all over you hear their tune.
Everybody rushing around; the day is coming soon.

Houses are decorated with lights; and don't forget the tree.
Stockings are hung and filled but something is bothering me.
There is one stocking empty, I know how very, very wrong,
Amid all the gifts and shopping and all the Christmas song.

It belongs to the most important one. Celebrating His birth.
With all the cheer and decorations, just what is their worth?
That special baby in his crib, lay in an undecorated barn.
Maybe you forgot that day; it is a cause for some alarm.

Would you give Him some of yourself, and say a prayer or two
That would help fill that empty stocking and be a part of you.
I too want to give my gift; it's filled with Love,
And thank Him for what He gives, that comes from way above.

By Mickey Deegan

LOVED ONES

This world is far from perfect, with bad things here and there;
There are good things, but the bad are very hard to bear.
Things happen in the world, different countries are affected too.
We always help and give them aid; Some appreciate it, but they are few.

We go about our work and business and try to smile,
Hoping things will get better in a little while,
But we now have trouble that hits us home.
It causes us to be sad and feel so all alone.

Loved one, family, and friends became quite ill.
There's no turning back for them, they're lost all their will.
We pray to God to help them; our hearts are ready to break.
We ask Him to stay close; to do it for their sake.

Whenever it's my time, I hope He'll take them and me to heaven above.
We'll be together again and have nothing but peace and love.

By Mickey Deegan

THE DHP

I've been going back and forth to DHP.
Looking for answers; the others and me.

We're searching for jobs, exploring our skills.
To be self-sufficient, working to pay our bills.

Martha and Sandy instruct us each day.
Trying to guide us for jobs with good pay.

They're reminding us too, how great we really are.
To bear our skills and just follow our star.

We're going to make it, and it's really great.
We're lucky to be women and it's never too late.

To reach our heights and be independent of men.
And know we ourselves are our very best friend.

There's no holding us back, highly we soar.
World out there... get ready ...swing open the door.

Here we come; we'll each take our place;
We're adding our talents to the human race.

We're going to be ready, gallant and brave,
And we thank the DHP for the help that it gave.

By Mickey Deegan

AMERICA'S DOMESTIC FOES

For America, we were once so very proud.
Her greatness and victories were shouted so loud.
But things seem so different now; things aren't that great.
In our country there's even some that hate.

There are some people stupidly in charge at the top.
Before it too late, they have to be stopped.
They don't love America the way the rest of us do.
What America does and stands for, they want to undo.

With God's help, and plenty of loyalty and fight,
Standing by her side, we'll keep her honor and might.
We're still real proud; just feeling a little low,
To realize she's got so many domestic foe.

Till the day their gone, we'll just have to bare,
All the wrongs they do that is so unfair.
How they got in charge, with ways so wrong;
They lied and cheated to us all along.

So many came from distant shores;
Trying to defeat our rules and mock our laws.
But Americans will stand and fight for her from within,
And like always, she'll be victorious and proudly win.

By Mickey Deegan

THE LUCKY FROG

I was just a lonely little frog.
Lots of people passed me by.
Sometimes I lay in plants and smog.
Sometimes, I would even cry.

A little person came my way.
He stopped to look me over.
It was a bright and sunny day,
And I sat surrounded by clover.

He picked me up and patted my head.
I didn't know right then,
I would always be free of dread,
And he would always be my friend.

I'm one little frog who was found
By a sweet and gentle boy.
My life to be ever surround
By love and lots of joy.

By Mickey Deegan

A POLICE OFFICER

What's a police officer, this you should know,
It's someone who cares, the way lives come and go,
It's one who believes in law and helping others
It's being kind to them, like sisters and brothers.

It's someone who's brave, expelling all fear
Showing the world, all they hold dear
Being right there when they're in need
Protecting others is their number one deed.

Some are hurt, some are even killed
All because they were heroically skilled,
The good people stand and try to watch their back,
While the bad people hide themselves and their evil track.

What would we do... Without a 911 call,
When one of us is hit, with a criminal fall.
Here they come...... the heroes in blue,
May God bless and protect each and every one of you.

By Mickey Deegan

"COMMON SENSE"

People who are book smart, certainly have a brain,
That will get them places and vocations they will gain
They can hold their heads up high and know they're doing their best,
They feel they're doing well and can pass any kind of test.

It does them very good and earned money can be great,
Book smart has its goals and certain kinds of fate,
Living that life will certainly be free of certain duress,
And most often free from lots of stress.

But being all they are, there is something lacking too,
They can't see it but we can... me and you,
Some don't have any common sense, which we all need,
How can they have hope, to ever be in the lead.

With common sense. It's a very different smart,
With life's troubles you can certainly take apart
You can settle struggles and be right there,
Always showing kindness and be very very fair.

It's having smartness, but not out of a book,
You don't have to read or even take a look.
It's naturally in you, commonly inside,
It shows your natural smartness, displaying real pride.

They both show smartness, from a book or from a heart,
But in this world, each one should play a big part,
Being book smart will never take the real place,
Of common sense facing this troubed world... right on face to face.

By Mickey Deegan

MICHELLE

Michelle now you're here, starting a new life,
Soon to be married and being a good wife,
I hope you'll be happy and greet everyday,
With your certain smile and in your special way.

Sometimes things aren't good, like all of us know,
Your happiness takes a turn and your feeling pretty low,
But now you have a special love that helps you handle all,
He'll be there to answer your every needed call.

When you say these special words meaning 'I do',
Let life open and realize, that you're a special you,
May you always be happy and play every card that's dealt,
Let all your happiness bloom and any troubles melt.

The best of everything

By Mickey Deegan

MY MAKER

Being I have my way, I know what I'd like to do,
To help others, especially all the people I knew,
My life wasn't easy, I tried to always stand tall,
Taking all the hits getting up, after each and every fall.

I tried to do my best, if needed I'd be there,
But sometimes I didn't know when I was meant to share,
I managed to go on though life was pretty tough,
I didn't know then that others too had it very rough.

I pray now for guidance, to be all that I can be,
Help me help others, especially those that depend on me,
Let me be in your service and try hard to do your will,
Help me help others, your wishes I'll try to fill.

I wish everyone served you, then life would be so serene,
Instead there's killing and violence and people very, very mean,
You always helped me JESUS, please stay here by my side,
To believe in you and follow you, fills me with such pride.

By Mickey Deegan

KIND AND NICE PEOPLE

I never had so many doors, open and close,
As I approach them in a silent pose,
If I drop something it was picked up,
Handed back to me with a great deal of luck.

If I found it hard to cross the street,
Someone came running whom I didn't even meet.
Sometimes it wasn't easy to get out of a chair,
Someone came running, with help to share.

I didn't know how, or try to explain,
All these people knew, about all my pain
So many people are as nice as they can be,
Now I know why....... my cane was walking with me.

By Mickey Deegan

YESTERYEAR

I never realized, how time would get away from me,
I never knew til now, how it would really be,
I didn't know how remembering, it would make me feel,
Just looking back and turning backwards the time wheel.

Music from the past, now makes me feel so very sad,
I didn't know, it would strike me this really bad.
Even all the old movies, makes me shed a tear,
Going way back to people and things of yesteryear.

My son Timmy and my sister Nancy left me, who I'll always love,
My constant prayer is to be back with them in heaven above,
I hope God hears me and listens, to all I got to say,
That all the people and things of yesteryear….. return to me one day.

By Mickey Deegan

"TURN AROUND"

There's someone behind you, for sometime,

Ever since you stole this heart of mine,

I tried to watch over all you do,

Times we see each other, are very few,

I'm waiting for the time, you'll stop and see,

Turn around and look....... Please notice me.

By Mickey Deegan

THE MICKEY DEEGAN POETRY COLLECTION

The book Mickey Deegan's Poetry Collection is about life, faith, patriotism, people, animals, love and politics as she sees it and lives it. There are poems for everyone and hoprefully to enjoy as much as she enjoyed writing them.

The author Mickey Deegan, is God – loving, patriotic and animal lover. She also loves people and has a great admiration for people who have earned it. Her passion is poetry, she's inpired to put her words on paper, most of her poems she has lived and describes her well.

www.ingramcontent.com/pod-product-compliance
Lightning Source LLC
Chambersburg PA
CBHW051006140626
46546CB00016B/1011